Cross the Bridge and Pass the Hedge

By Cameron Macintosh

Mitch, Jace and Mum set off
to visit Pop at his lodge.

They like to walk from home
to Pop's lodge.

There is a lot to see along the way!

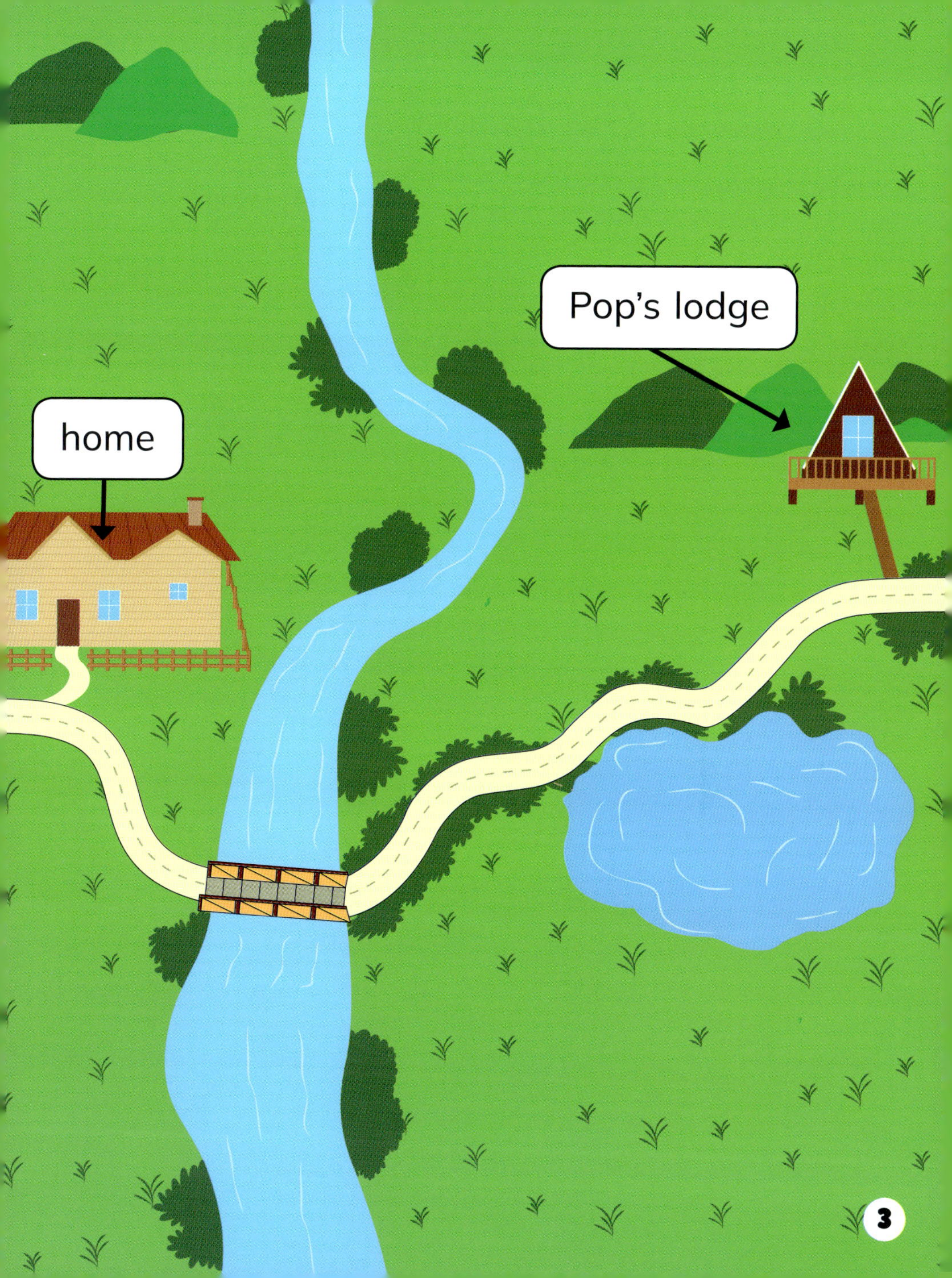
Pop's lodge
home

To get to the lodge,
they must cross a long bridge.

Sometimes they see fish in the water under the bridge.

They also see birds by the edge of the stream.

Once they cross the bridge,
they go past a hedge.

The hedge is long.

Mitch runs his hand along the edge of the hedge.

Past the hedge,
Mum and the kids come to a lake.

Mitch and Jace like to skip stones from the edge of this lake.

Mitch's stone skips three times.

Jace's stone skips five or six times.

It's a lot of fun!

This is the hard part of the walk!

They trudge up and up this hill to reach Pop's lodge.

They are almost there!

Pop's lodge is on the ridge of the hill.

"You are here!" said Pop,
with a smile.
"I have fudge cake in the fridge."

They all have a big wedge of cake!

Yum!

Back home they go!

Down the hill,
past the lake,
along the hedge
and across the bridge.

See you next time, Pop!

CHECKING FOR MEANING

1. Why do Mitch, Jace and Mum like to walk to Pop's lodge? *(Literal)*
2. What did Mitch and Jace do at the edge of the lake? *(Literal)*
3. Do you think Pop was expecting the visit from Mum and the kids? Why? *(Inferential)*
4. Was it a good idea for Mitch, Jace and Mum to walk to Pop's? Why? *(Evaluative)*

EXTENDING VOCABULARY

lodge	What does the word *lodge* mean in the text? What other word could the author have used instead of *lodge*? What makes a lodge different from other houses?
hedge	Look at the word *hedge*. How many letters are in this word? How many sounds? What is a hedge made of?
skip	What did Mitch and Jace skip in the text? What else might you skip? Use *skip* in a sentence of your own to show its meaning.

MOVING BEYOND THE TEXT

1. Do you like going for walks and spending time in nature? Why?
2. Have you ever skipped rocks? What do you think you need to know and do to be a good rock-skipper?
3. What kind of food would you prepare if you had friends or family coming to visit?
4. What other activities can you do at a lake or park?

TIME TO WRITE

Write about a time you've gone for a walk somewhere. Where did you go? What did you see along the way?